PRICKLY
AND
POISONOUS

The deadly defenses of nature's strangest animals and plants

Written by
Anita Ganeri

READER'S DIGEST
Kids®

Westport, Connecticut

A Reader's Digest Kids Book

Published by Reader's Digest Young Families, Inc.

Produced by Marshall Editions

Library of Congress Cataloging in Publication Data

Ganeri, Anita. 1961–
   Prickly and poisonous : the deadly defenses of nature's strangest animals and plants / written by Anita Ganeri.
      p. cm.
   Includes index.
   Summary: Examines how various animals, fish, birds, insects, and different plants protect themselves from danger.
      ISBN 0-89577-696-0
      1. Animal weapons—Juvenile literature.   2. Animal defenses—Juvenile literature.   3. Plant defenses—Juvenile literature.
   [1. Plant defenses.] I. Title.
   QL940.G35 1995
   591.57—dc20   95-8801
                                                                CIP
                                                                 AC

Editors:	Charlotte Evans, Kate Phelps, Cynthia O'Brien
Designers:	Stephen Woosnam-Savage, Ralph Pitchford, Branka Surla
Consultant:	Dr. Philip Whitfield
Researchers:	Liz Ferguson, Jon Richards
Production:	Janice Storr, Angela Kew

Marshall Editions would like to thank the following artists for illustrating this book:

Joanne Cowne 18–19, 34–35, 36–37, 40–41
Bernard Robinson 10–11, 14–15, 24–25
Eric Robson (Garden Studio) 8–9, 12–13, 16–17, 22–23, 26–27, 32–33, 42–43
Colin Woolf (Linda Rogers Associates) 20–21, 28–29, 30–31, 38–39

Cover artwork: **Eric Robson**
Cover designer: **Michael Harnden**

10 9 8 7 6 5 4 3 2 1

Originated by Master Image, Singapore
Printed and bound in Italy by Officine Grafiche de Agostini-Novara

CONTENTS

PUFFERFISH

There are some 120 species of pufferfish living in tropical oceans around the world. These fish get their name from their very special method of self-defense. If danger threatens, a pufferfish gulps in air and water and inflates its body until it looks like a small, round balloon, two or three times its normal size. When puffed up, it is too large for all but the biggest predators to bite or swallow. The skin of some pufferfish is also covered in sharp spines that stick up when the fish is inflated. As soon as the danger is past, the pufferfish quickly deflates and returns to its usual shape and size.

Some pufferfish have extremely poisonous internal organs, such as the heart, liver, and intestines. The tiniest taste of these can kill a person in minutes. In Japan, however, raw pufferfish, or *fugu*, is considered a great delicacy. Chefs remove the poisonous parts and slice the flesh into wafer-thin pieces. Despite the careful preparation, about 20 people a year die in Japan from eating pufferfish.

When a pufferfish inflates its body, hungry predators, such as this conger eel, are scared away by the sudden change in size or put off by the sharp spines.

Bandtail pufferfish
This pufferfish lives in the Atlantic Ocean, where it keeps to the shallow water along the coasts. Its body is covered with tiny spines.

Oceanic pufferfish
This poisonous pufferfish is found in the Atlantic, Indian, and Pacific oceans, where it lives near the surface, out in the open sea.

Common pufferfish
This pufferfish lives in the rivers of India, Burma, and Malaysia. It is one of only a few types of freshwater pufferfish. It is poisonous and can inflate its body into a ball, but it does not have a spiny skin.

The spines on the body of the pufferfish are made from the same material as fish scales. They normally lie flat, but stick up all over when the fish puffs itself up. Without this defense, the slow-swimming pufferfish would be very vulnerable to predators.

Porcupine fish

The porcupine fish gets its name from the long, sharp spines all over its skin. It can inflate its body to the size of a soccer ball if danger threatens. Porcupine fish live in warm, tropical areas of the Pacific, Indian, and Atlantic oceans.

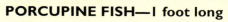

PORCUPINE FISH—1 foot long

Pufferfish eat crabs, sea urchins, sea stars, and other shellfish. They crush and grind the hard shells with their beaklike mouths. This "beak" can be sharp enough to bite a person's finger off!

9

A porcupine is covered with 20,000 to 30,000 sharp-tipped quills on its back and tail. Porcupines are born with a full set of quills. These are soft at first but harden within two weeks.

CRESTED PORCUPINE—
3 feet from nose to tail

Among the porcupine's main enemies are hyenas, lions, and leopards. These animals have learned how to flip the porcupine onto its back, exposing its soft, unprotected belly.

Porcupines come out at night to look for roots, fruit, and berries to eat. During the day, they sleep in burrows or cracks in the rock. Baby porcupines are born in grass-lined burrows under ground.

PORCUPINES

Porcupines are rodents, related to guinea pigs and chinchillas. But they have one special feature that makes them stand out—the thousands of needle-sharp quills or spines covering their bodies. Porcupines use their quills for self-defense. First, they try to frighten an enemy away by stamping their feet and then grunting and shaking their tails so that their quills rattle. If this display fails, a porcupine rushes at its enemy and lashes out at it with its prickly tail. The quills are not poisonous but some stick in the enemy's skin, causing a sharp pain and a nasty wound. People used to think that porcupines could take aim and fire their quills at an enemy. This isn't true, but the quills are powerful weapons all the same.

There are more than 20 species of porcupines. Those that live in North and South America spend much of their time up in the trees, searching for food. They are excellent climbers, with feet and tails designed for gripping. The porcupines of Europe, Asia, and Africa forage for food on the forest floor. Both types are mainly vegetarian.

Crested porcupine
These porcupines are found in southern Europe, Africa, and Asia. Their hollow quills grow up to one foot in length. If threatened, the porcupine rushes backward into its enemy, such as this jackal. Its sharp quills break off easily, and a few are left behind in the victim's skin.

Prehensile-tailed porcupine
This porcupine lives in the forests of South America. It uses its long, flexible tail as an extra hand for gripping branches as it climbs and feeds.

North American porcupine
This porcupine lives in the forests of Canada and the United States. It climbs trees to find leaves, twigs, nuts, and berries. In summer it spends more time on the ground feeding on flowers and fruit.

SEA URCHINS

Sea urchins belong to a group of sea animals called echinoderms, which means "spiny-skinned." Apart from sea urchins, the group includes sea stars, brittle stars, sea cucumbers, and sea lilies. There are about 800 species of sea urchins. They come in a variety of shapes and sizes, from oval shaped to disk and globe shaped.

Sea urchins are covered in a hard casing and a mass of prickly spines, which they use for moving about, burrowing, and self-defense. The spines are often poisonous and can inflict painful wounds on enemies, including humans. They break off easily in the flesh of a victim and are very hard to remove because of their barbed edges. Sea urchins also have rows of small, hollow organs, known as tube feet. These are used for walking on the sea floor, attaching themselves to rocks, collecting food, and sensing the world about them. Some types of sea urchins, such as sea potatoes, use their spines to burrow into the sand on the seabed.

A sea urchin's skin is sensitive to light and dark. If an enemy swims by, casting a shadow, the urchin's spines swivel around, ready to be used for self-defense.

Black sea urchin
The shrimpfish's long, thin, striped body helps it to hide among a black sea urchin's spines. This keeps it safe from hungry predators.

The long-spined red sea urchin feeds on algae and on small sea creatures, such as sponges. Its enemies include the triggerfish, which is not deterred by its needle-sharp spines.

Cidaris cidaris
This spectacular sea urchin lives in deep water in the Mediterranean Sea and north Atlantic Ocean. Its body is protected by long, pointed spines, each surrounded by smaller, flatter spines.

Flower urchin
A flower urchin is covered in tiny pincers that look like small flower petals but are in fact highly poisonous if touched. It uses the poison for self-defense.

The color of the long-spined red sea urchin helps to camouflage it because, under the water, red seems darker than black. It often hides during the day, coming out to feed at night.

12

Long-spined red sea urchin
Living among the rocky coral reefs in warm, tropical seas around the world, this sea urchin is easily identified by its dramatic covering of long, red spines. In some species of long-spined urchins, these spines can reach a foot in length.

LONG-SPINED RED SEA URCHIN—spines about 8 inches long

13

ECHIDNAS

There are two types of echidnas, or spiny anteaters—the long-beaked and the short-beaked. Both live solely in Australia and nearby islands. Echidnas belong to an extremely unusual group of mammals, known as monotremes. Together with the duck-billed platypus, they are the only mammals that lay eggs. The eggs have soft, leathery shells. The under-developed young hatch after about 10 days, then suckle their mother's milk.

Echidnas use their long, thin snouts to sniff out and probe for food, which they dig up with their powerful claws. They lap up their prey of ants, termites, and other insects with their long, sticky tongues. A short-beaked echidna can stick its tongue out seven inches or more! Echidnas do not have teeth for chewing their food but have horny plates in the roofs of their mouths for grinding. To protect themselves, they have a coat of thick fur and spines that are sharp enough to pierce leather.

These animals spend much of their time on their own. In hot weather, echidnas hunt for food at night when it is cooler, but during the winter they hunt by day. Some echidnas, especially those that live in mountain areas, hibernate in very cold weather. At other times, they rest in hollow logs or under large piles of leaves. They dig burrows for raising their young.

Long-beaked echidna
This echidna is bigger than its short-beaked relative, with shorter spines and a longer snout.

SHORT-BEAKED ECHIDNA—
17 inches long

14

Echidnas use their spines for self-defense, and they can curl up into a prickly ball for extra protection. The spines are made of the same material as hair.

1. Adults mate.

BEARING YOUNG
Echidnas mate between June and August, and the female lays a single egg in her pouch. The baby hatches and suckles its mother's milk. It leaves the pouch after three weeks, when its spines begin to grow.

2. The female lays an egg (enlarged in inset picture).

3. The baby grows inside the mother's pouch (shown in closeup).

Short-beaked echidna
This echidna is found in Australia, Tasmania, and New Guinea. It has a browny-black coat with long spines on its back and sides. It uses its claws to dig burrows to hide in if danger threatens. It can disappear from view in a matter of seconds, as if it has sunk into the ground.

PLANTS

Because they are a major source of food for animals and people, plants are in constant danger of being eaten. As a result, many plants have developed special weapons, such as prickles, thorns, and stingers to fend off their enemies. An animal that has taken a mouthful of prickly thistle or had its nose stung is unlikely to attack again. Other plants survive because they are poisonous or unpleasant to eat. Some trees only produce poison in their leaves when they are actually under attack. They also release a type of gas which alerts neighboring trees to make the same poison so that their leaves are inedible too.

A few plants use their prickles or spines for purposes other than self-defense. The Venus's-flytrap, one of a few meat-eating plants, uses the spikes on its leaves to help it trap insects.

Indian millet

Sorghum, or Indian millet, is one of the world's most important food crops. It is grown in Asia, Africa, and South America, where the grain is ground into flour for making a type of bread. But the leaves of Indian millet contain poisonous cyanide which fends off grazing animals. The poison only becomes active when an animal takes a bite of a leaf.

Spear thistle

Thistles grow wild in fields, by roadsides, and on waste ground. With their spiny stems, spiky leaves, and prickly flowers, they are among the best protected of plants. Most hungry animals keep well away from thistles—they are just too painful to eat! Although larger animals are warned off by the thistle's prickles, tiny insects, such as aphids, feed in their thousands on thistle sap. People, too, have eaten thistles for hundreds of years, but they cook the plants to make them softer.

Saguaro cactus

Like all cactuses, the saguaro has no leaves. Instead it has a thick stem which loses less water than wide leaves would, thus enabling it to adapt to hot, dry desert conditions. Cactuses have sharp spines to deter thirsty animals from nibbling on the stem to reach the store of water inside. The saguaro is the biggest cactus in the cactus family and, despite its spines, owls and woodpeckers make their nests in its stem.

Stinging nettle

Nettles have tiny bristly stingers (shown in closeup) on their leaves. If an animal touches the nettle, the stingers stick into its skin and release a poisonous liquid into the animal's body. The poison causes a painful rash on the skin. The scientific name for a nettle, *Urtica dioica*, comes from the Latin word *uro*, which means "I burn."

Foxglove

Many woods or areas of scrubland are brightened up by pink spires of foxglove flowers. Foxglove leaves contain a strong poison, called digitalis. In large doses, it can cause dizziness, heart tremors, and even heart failure. In small measures, however, the same poison is an important medicine and is used to treat people with heart problems. In this way, foxgloves have saved millions of lives.

Holly

Holly bushes grow in woods and hedges all over Europe and North America. Their shiny, evergreen leaves are edged with sharp, prickly spikes that help to protect them from animal attack, especially in winter, when food is scarce. The leaves near the bottom of the bush are more prickly than those higher up because they are at greater risk of being eaten.

Venus's-flytrap

The amazing Venus's-flytrap grows only in the southern United States. It uses the spikes on the edges of its leaves not for self-defense, but for catching food. The two halves of a leaf are joined together by a hinge. On each surface there are also a number of stiff bristles. When an insect brushes against these bristles, it sets the leaf trap in motion. In less than a second, the trap snaps shut and the spikes interlock, imprisoning the insect. The insect's body is dissolved and digested by chemicals inside the leaf. The trap then opens again, ready to catch another meal.

17

CATERPILLARS

A juicy, plump caterpillar crawling slowly across a leaf makes a tempting snack for a passing bird, which will eat the caterpillar or carry it back to its nest to feed to its young. To avoid or lessen the chances of being eaten, caterpillars have developed a variety of defenses. Some are camouflaged by their color or shape to look like leaves, twigs, or even bird droppings. They blend in perfectly with their backgrounds and are well hidden from enemies.

Other caterpillars are equipped with quite different defenses. Their particular colors, such as black, white, orange, or yellow, warn potential attackers that they are poisonous if eaten and are best left alone. Other poisonous caterpillars are covered in tufts of hairy spines. These spines can be used to inject poison into predators or, at the least, can cause an irritating rash if they are touched.

Saddleback caterpillar
This caterpillar has on its sides tufts of short, poisonous bristles that sting if touched.

Emperor gum moth caterpillar
This moth lives in Australia and some areas of New Zealand. The caterpillars grow to about three inches long, while adult moths have a wingspan of nearly five inches. Emperor gum moth caterpillars are covered in sharp spines that cause a rash if they are touched.

EMPEROR GUM MOTH CATERPILLAR
Shown at actual size—about 3 inches

Most birds and other predators learn to avoid hairy caterpillars, because they are often poisonous or unpleasant to eat.

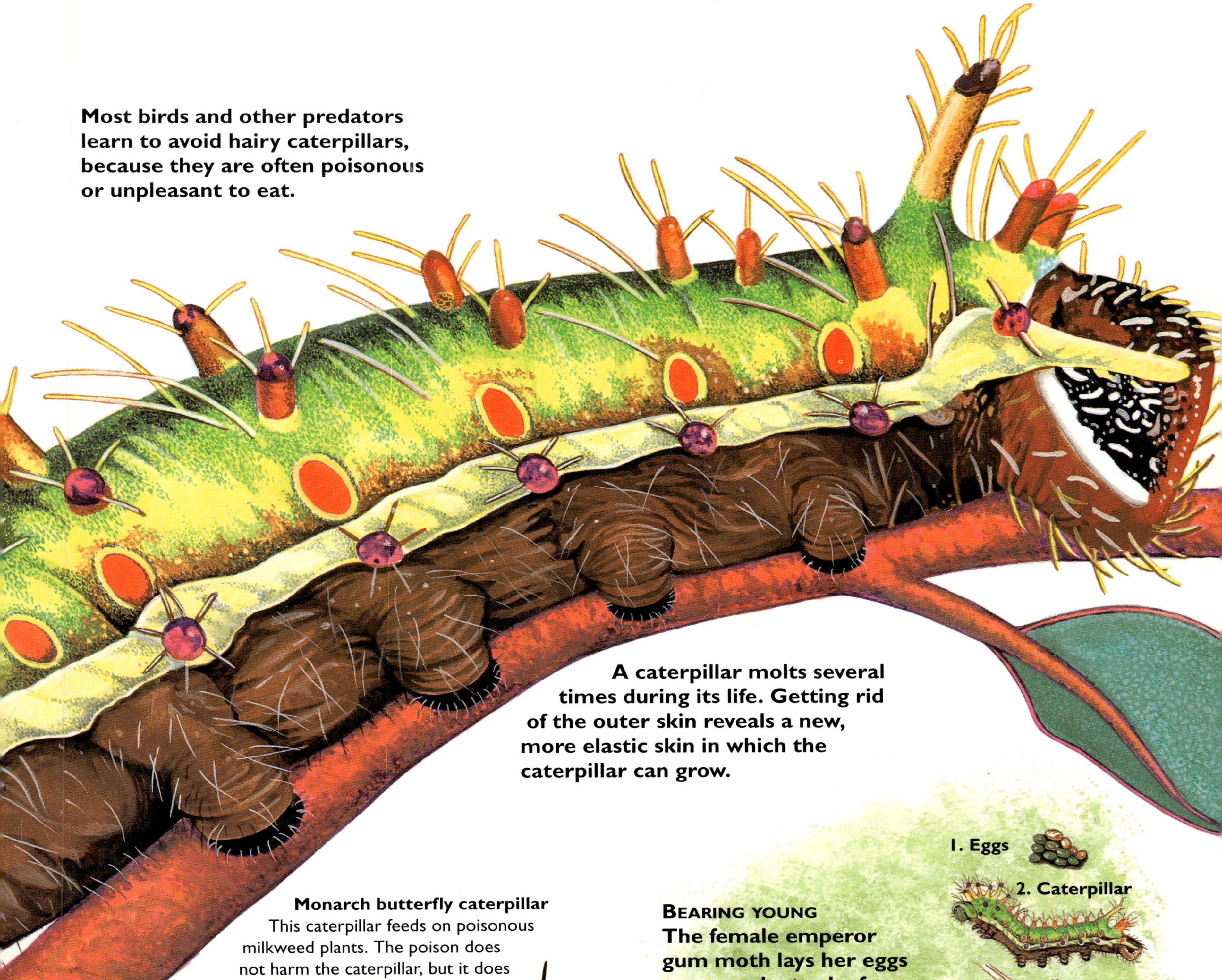

A caterpillar molts several times during its life. Getting rid of the outer skin reveals a new, more elastic skin in which the caterpillar can grow.

Monarch butterfly caterpillar
This caterpillar feeds on poisonous milkweed plants. The poison does not harm the caterpillar, but it does make it taste horrible to birds.

Cracker butterfly caterpillar
The cracker caterpillar is found in Central America. Its long, black spines are poisonous.

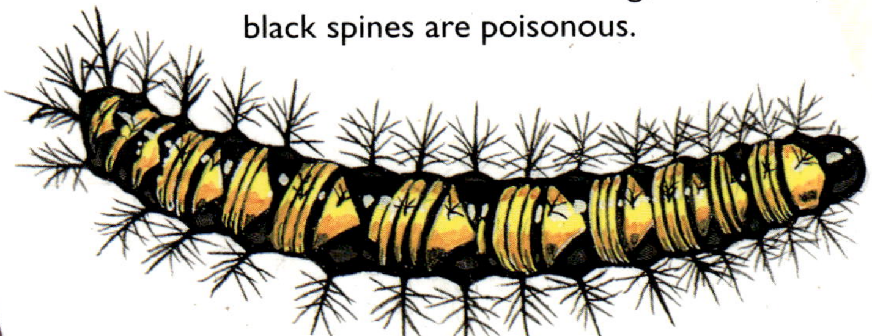

BEARING YOUNG
The female emperor gum moth lays her eggs on a eucalyptus leaf. These hatch into large caterpillars which feed and grow and then spin silk cocoons around themselves. It takes from one to five years inside the cocoon for the adult moth to emerge.

1. Eggs

2. Caterpillar

3. Cocoon

4. Adult moth

19

Gila monster

The gila monster lives in the deserts of the United States and Mexico. It feeds on birds and small mammals, which it kills with a poisonous bite and swallows whole. It also eats birds' eggs. It stores fat in its tail and lives off this in winter when food is scarce. If threatened, the gila monster rears up and huffs and puffs. If this does not work, it bites!

Princely mastigure

This lizard uses its thick tail to protect itself from attackers. If an enemy comes too close, the lizard lashes out with its tail, which is studded with sharp, painful spikes. The princely mastigure lives in Africa. It eats mainly leaves, grass, fruit, and flowers.

LIZARDS

Lizards use a wide range of defense mechanisms to protect themselves from their enemies. Some simply scurry away as fast as they can. Others shed their tails to distract hungry predators. (They later grow new tails to replace them.) Some are perfectly camouflaged to blend in with their surroundings and can even change color as they move from place to place. But the thorny devil is one of the most remarkable lizards of all. It has an amazing spiny coat to keep it safe from predators.

There are only two types of poisonous lizards—the gila monster and its close relative, the Mexican beaded lizard. Both have heavy bodies with brightly colored, beadlike scales on their backs. When the gila monster bites, poison from glands in its lower jaw flows down grooves in its teeth and is chewed into the wound. These lizards mainly use their poison for killing prey but will strike in self-defense if they are provoked. The poison attacks the victim's nervous system, causing paralysis and terrible pain. It is very effective on small mammals and birds, but it works less well on other reptiles and frogs. The bite is rarely fatal to human beings and very few people have ever been bitten.

Thorny devil

This incredible-looking lizard lives in the dry, sandy deserts of Australia. It wanders slowly along, on the lookout for ants and termites to eat, protected from attack by its prickles. The female thorny devil lays her eggs in November or December. The newly hatched young are miniature versions of their parents, complete with spikes.

Despite its fearsome looks, the thorny devil is quite harmless. It laps up ants and termites with its long tongue and can eat as many as 1,000 ants in a single meal.

The thorny devil is covered from head to foot in sharp spikes. These protect it from attack and are also useful for collecting water. Dew settles on the spikes and trickles down into the lizard's mouth.

21

WASPS AND BEES

Wasps and bees use poisonous stingers to defend themselves or to catch prey. The stinger is a long, hollow, pointed tube that pumps poison into a victim. The poison is made up of different chemicals and causes a painful red swelling. Insect stings are not normally fatal to people unless the person concerned is allergic to the poison. Wasps have smooth, unbarbed stingers that can be pulled out of the skin and used again. But bees have barbed stingers that stick in the skin and cannot be pulled out. In using its sting, a bee badly wounds itself and soon dies.

Like many poisonous creatures, most wasps and bees are boldly colored. Their vivid colors—usually yellow and black—warn their enemies that they can be stung. Some harmless insects, such as hoverflies and hornet moths, mimic these colors to fool their enemies into leaving them alone. Wasps and bees will usually sting only if you pester them. If a wasp starts buzzing around you, stand still and stay calm. It will soon fly off again. Some wasps and bees live in large groups and will sometimes launch a mass attack if their nest or hive is disturbed.

The wasp's stinger is in fact its modified ovipositor, the organ it uses to lay eggs. This means that it is only the female that can sting. The thread-waisted wasp uses her stinger to paralyze prey. Bees and many other wasps use their stingers in self-defense.

BEARING YOUNG

A thread-waisted wasp first digs a burrow, then flies off to find a caterpillar. She stings the caterpillar to paralyze it and drags it back to her burrow. Here she lays an egg on the caterpillar and seals the burrow. When the wasp grub hatches, it feasts on the caterpillar.

1. The female digs a burrow.

2. A caterpillar is taken back to the burrow.

3. An egg is laid on the caterpillar.

Mining bee
Bees only use their stingers to fend off predators. Unlike the thread-waisted wasp, the female mining bee digs a nest in the ground and stocks it with balls of pollen and nectar to feed her young.

Sandhills hornet
This type of wasp builds round paper nests in trees or under roof eaves. If a nest is disturbed, the hornets will attack and viciously sting the intruder.

THREAD-WASTED WASP
Shown at actual size—about 1½ inches

Thread-waisted wasp
These wasps live in the United States and Canada. They use their poison to provide food for their newly hatched grubs. The poison is used to paralyze insects and caterpillars, not to kill them. This ensures that the meat stays fresh. When the grubs have eaten the prey, the female will bring them further supplies.

Thousands of wasp species use poison to capture prey. A South American wasp even stings huge, bird-eating spiders. It then bites the spider's legs off to make it easier to carry to its burrow!

STINGRAYS

Stingrays belong to a group of fish known as rays. Sharks, skates, and rays are all related, forming a family of fish that have skeletons made of gristly cartilage rather than of bone. Rays often lie on the seabed, where their flat shape and coloring make them very difficult to see. Although many rays are harmless, some will quickly attack if they are stepped on or disturbed.

Stingrays are found in warm, tropical waters around the world. They get their name from the sharp spines that grow near the base of their long, thin tails. The spines are dangerous weapons. If an enemy gets too close, the stingray whips its tail around and drives the spine into its victim's body. The spine is coated with poison and inflicts an extremely painful, though rarely fatal, wound. Several human swimmers have died after being stung in the chest or stomach by stingrays. Stingray spines were once used by local people as weapons and are sometimes unfortunately sold as letter openers to tourists.

Eagle ray
These rays grow to about six feet in width. They swim fast through the water, flapping their huge, pointed fins like wings. They find their prey on the seabed by squirting water out of their mouths to blow away the sand.

24

Southern stingray
This stingray lives along the Atlantic coast of the United States, Central America, and the Caribbean. It usually lies on the seabed, half-buried in the sand. Here it feeds on scraps of fish, crabs, and shellfish that it sucks in and crushes with its strong teeth.

The stingray's side fins are shaped like triangular wings. The ray flaps them gently up and down as it swims, almost as if it is flying under water.

Atlantic torpedo ray
Torpedo rays use electric shocks to stun or kill their prey. The shock would be strong enough to throw a human to the ground.

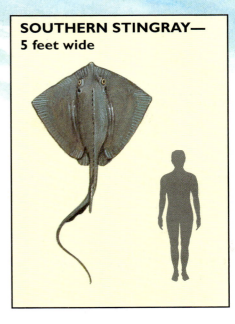

SOUTHERN STINGRAY—
5 feet wide

SCORPION FISH

The scorpion fish family has about 300 members. Some are boldly colored, like the lionfish, to warn enemies. Others, such as the deadly stonefish, are superbly camouflaged, blending in with the seabed. Stonefish are very difficult to see, and their poison is strong enough to kill a person unlucky enough to step on one.

Swimming slowly through a tropical coral reef, the lionfish is a spectacular sight. But its beautiful, striped fins hide a range of dangerous weapons. Each fin is equipped with sharp spines that inject a powerful dose of poison into any attacker. The poison can be very painful but is not usually fatal. Lionfish use their poison in self-defense, not to catch prey. In some places, lionfish are eaten as a delicacy. Their spines have to be removed extremely carefully because they can still sting even after the fish is dead.

Rascasse
This scorpion fish has a row of poisonous spines along its back for self-defense. It lurks among the seaweed in shallow coastal waters.

BURIED TERROR
A stonefish's warty skin is disguised with bits of coral, mud, and algae. Buried on the seabed, it is very hard to see. If threatened, it raises the spines on its back. These are sharp enough to inject a poison, even through rubber-soled shoes.

1. The fish chooses a site.

2. Here it half-buries itself in the sand.

3. Any small fish that swims by is quickly swallowed.

The lionfish can afford to swim slowly and leisurely through the reef. Thanks to its poisonous spines, it has very few enemies. Lionfish themselves feed on crabs, shrimp, and other small fish.

Lionfish

This beautiful fish lives in the warm waters of the Indian and Pacific oceans, where it drifts among the coral reefs. Its brilliant stripes are a clear warning to other fish to stay well away from its poisonous spines. Lionfish are sometimes also known as dragonfish or zebrafish.

The lionfish's poisonous spines are found on its long fanlike fins. If threatened, the lionfish spreads out its fins and inflicts a painful sting with its spines.

MENAGERIE

An animal's life is full of danger. On the one hand, it must go out and hunt for food and on the other, it must avoid becoming a meal for another hungry creature. This is where prickles and poisons are at their most useful. Spines, spikes, and sharp prickles will deter most predators. Poisons and chemicals can be used for warning off predators and for killing prey to eat. Many poisonous animals are greatly feared, but little understood by human beings. Very few are lethal to us and most people are only bitten or stung through their own carelessness. The lives of these animals are fascinating, and on these two pages you will find a collection, or menagerie, of some of the best-known and more unusual prickly and poisonous creatures.

Centipede

The centipede is a secretive animal, lurking by day in damp places under stones and logs and coming out at night to search for food. It is a fierce hunter and can move very quickly. Its large jaws are hidden behind the first pair of legs. These legs are modified to form poison fangs for killing prey. Tropical centipedes can grow up to a foot in length and have bitten humans, though never fatally.

Hooded pitohui

This bird lives in the mountains and jungles of New Guinea. Until recently, scientists thought that there were no poisonous birds, but then it was discovered that the feathers, skin, and flesh of some species of pitohui contain a poison strong enough to kill frogs and mice. In humans, the poison causes numbness, burning, and sneezing. The pitohui probably uses its poison to deter feather lice as well as reptiles, which prey on its young.

Scorpion

These animals are famous for the stingers in their tails. They are nocturnal creatures— during the day they hide under logs or stones. They use their stingers mainly for self-defense but will also sting prey if it is large or struggles too much. The scorpion's poison first paralyzes, then kills its victim. Scorpions catch their prey in their large claws. Insects and spiders are their main source of food, but large scorpions also eat lizards and mice. Most are not dangerous to humans, although some scorpion species have poison as powerful as that of a cobra and are capable of killing a person. They usually sting only if they are annoyed. There are about 650 different species of scorpions, ranging in size from about half an inch to seven inches. The scorpion shown here is the black emperor.

Cone shell

Cone shells are found in the warm tropical waters of the Indian and Pacific oceans and are among the deadliest sea creatures. They usually eat fish or worms, which they spear with their harpoonlike teeth. Then they inject a powerful poison. This paralyzes the prey, which is swallowed whole. The beautiful shells of these mollusks are highly prized by collectors, even though some unwary shell collectors have been fatally harpooned. The poison is said to be able to kill a person in 15 minutes.

Shrew

The shrew is a small, mouselike creature with short, thick fur and a long, pointed snout. Shrews are found all over the world. They feed mainly on insects and other small animals, such as slugs and earthworms. Several species of shrews have a poisonous bite that they use to kill their prey. The poison is produced by their salivary glands and injected into their prey when they bite. The short-tailed shrew's poison is strong enough to kill a frog in just a few seconds. Shrews and their close relations, solenodons, are the only mammals with a poisonous bite.

Hedgehog

This prickly creature is covered in a coat of sharp spines, formed from the same material as hair. An adult hedgehog's coat is made up of about 5,000 spines. When a hedgehog is threatened, muscles at the base of each spine pull them upright, while other muscles in the hedgehog's body allow it to curl up into a tight, prickly ball to protect its soft belly. Very few creatures would attempt to tackle such a bundle of spikes. The hedgehog's main enemy is the car. Thousands are killed on roads each year. Baby hedgehogs are born complete with soft spines, although these do not break through the skin for several hours. There are 14 species of hedgehogs found in most parts of Europe, Asia, and Africa. Shown here is the European species.

29

SNAKES

All snakes are meat eaters, feeding on animals ranging from mice, birds, and frogs to antelopes and alligators. Some snakes, the boa constrictors, kill their prey by squeezing it to death. Others, such as cobras, taipans, vipers, and rattlesnakes, use deadly poisons. In many cases, the snake bites its victim and injects poison into it through two long, hollow teeth, called fangs. Then it swallows its prey whole.

Snake poison is a mixture of chemicals and is made in the snake's salivary glands. Some 35,000 people worldwide die of snakebites every year—just a teaspoon of cobra poison could kill 80 people. But don't be alarmed: only about 50 of the 2,700 species of snakes are poisonous to people, and snakes will usually attack only if provoked—they prefer to slither off and hide. Many people bitten by snakes can be treated with an antivenom.

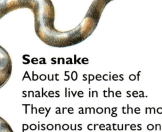

Coral snake
This snake's bold colors warn that it is highly poisonous. Some harmless snakes mimic these colors to scare off predators.

Sea snake
About 50 species of snakes live in the sea. They are among the most poisonous creatures on Earth—many are far more deadly than land snakes.

BEARING YOUNG
Some snakes, such as the taipan, lay eggs. The baby snake cuts its way out of the egg using a sharp "egg tooth" on its upper lip. Other snakes, including the rattlesnake, give birth to live young.

3. The baby snakes hatch out of the eggs.

2. The female buries the eggs.

1. The adult taipans mate.

To warn enemies that it is about to strike, a rattlesnake shakes the rattle at the tip of its tail. This makes an eerie buzzing sound. The rattle is formed by rings of hollow scales, loosely locked together.

Eastern diamondback rattlesnake
The largest of all rattlesnakes, the Eastern diamondback is the most dangerous snake in the United States. It lives in woods and farmland, where its diamond-patterned skin helps to camouflage it among the vegetation as it lies in wait for prey such as birds and rabbits.

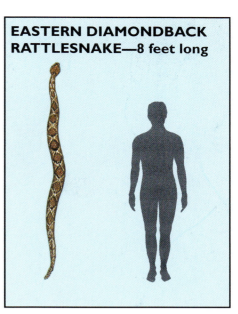

EASTERN DIAMONDBACK RATTLESNAKE—8 feet long

Snakes inject poison through fangs that are replaced every few months. The poison causes heart failure in their victims.

Experts think that snakes may be able to adjust the amount of venom they use to kill prey. If the prey is a large, strong animal, the snake pumps in more venom. A snake has to swallow its prey whole because, with only two fangs, it cannot bite chunks out of its food.

Many jellyfish are strong swimmers, but the Portuguese man-of-war has a float that drifts on the water. This float gives it its name because it looks a bit like an old Portuguese warship.

Portuguese man-of-war
These amazing creatures are found in warm oceans all around the world. Their long tentacles can trail up to 165 feet behind the body, but most average about 50 feet. A Portuguese man-of-war is not one single animal but is made up of hundreds of tiny separate animals! Each has a specific job to do. Some help it to float, others sting prey, and yet others digest food.

Sea wasp
This jellyfish is one of the world's most dangerous creatures. A single sea wasp has 40 million stinging cells. It can kill a person in two to three minutes.

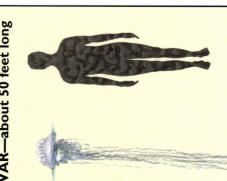

PORTUGUESE MAN-OF-WAR—about 50 feet long

JELLYFISH

Jellyfish and their close relations—the Portuguese man-of-war, sea anemones, and corals—all share one special feature. They have tentacles loaded with stinging cells that they use to poison their prey. The poison used by the Portuguese man-of-war is extremely strong (about three-quarters as powerful as an Indian cobra's poison) and can kill a fish in seconds. In humans, it causes a sharp, burning pain, but is rarely fatal.

Jellyfish trail their tentacles through the water. If a fish brushes past them, it triggers the stinging cells into action. Each shoots a sharp, barbed spine loaded with poison into the fish's body to paralyze it. The jellyfish also sends out sticky threads to help entangle its prey. Then the tentacles pull the fish into the jellyfish's mouth.

Coral polyps
Coral reefs are built up by animals called coral polyps. Polyps use their stingers to trap tiny creatures for food and as a means of self-defense.

Sea anemones and clownfish
Protected by a coating of slimy mucus, the clownfish lives among a tropical sea anemone's stinging tentacles, safe from predators.

In spite of their stinging tentacles, jellyfish and their close relatives are eaten by certain animals that are not affected by their poison. Even the Portuguese man-of-war is eaten by a sea slug that keeps the stingers to use as weapons of its own.

BEETLES

Many types of beetles use poisonous chemicals to deter potential predators and to kill their prey. Some beetles use poison to make their bodies taste horrible, while others have lethal weapons. In common with many other poisonous animals, they advertise the fact by the bold warning colors of red, orange, yellow, and black. Their message is clear: "Keep away!"

The larvae (young) of some African leaf beetles are so poisonous that local people use them to tip their hunting arrows. Other beetles squirt out jets of poisonous spray that can cause burns, blisters, and even blindness. The bombardier beetle has one of the most effective defense mechanisms. If provoked, it shoots a boiling-hot spray of poisonous chemicals from its abdomen, straight at its attacker. Darkling beetles also squirt poisonous chemicals from their abdomens, but not quite as successfully. Some mice have found a way to avoid the spray. A mouse snatches a beetle and rams its rear end into the soil where it discharges the poison harmlessly. The mouse then eats the beetle from the head down.

Darkling beetle
If attacked, some species of darkling beetles stand head down, tail up, and squirt a poisonous spray at their enemy.

Ladybug
A ladybug's bright colors warn its enemies to leave it alone. If attacked, it oozes vile-tasting sticky, yellow blood from its knees. This gums up the attacker's mouth and sends it hurrying away.

Toxic oil beetle
This beetle contains a strong poison that people can extract and use in medicines. It has bright warning colors.

34

The poison sprayed by the bombardier beetle consists of chemicals called quinones. These are produced in a "combustion chamber" inside the beetle's body. They are forced out with a loud "pop."

Bombardier beetle
This beetle lives near ponds, rivers, and lakes in North America, Africa, and Asia. Its striking coloring warns would-be predators to keep their distance. The beetle gets its name from its extraordinary defense mechanism. If attacked, it "bombards" its enemy with a spray of chemicals.

BOMBARDIER BEETLE— ½ inch long

Shown at actual size

A bombardier beetle can swivel the tip of its abdomen around in order to fire its poison spray more accurately into its attacker's face. It can continue spraying for some time before its store is used up.

AMPHIBIANS

Amphibians are creatures such as frogs, toads, newts, and salamanders that spend part of their lives on land and part in the water. Amphibians have many enemies. Their soft, protein-packed bodies make them ideal meals for birds, mammals, and snakes.

If possible, an amphibian under attack tries to avoid a fight and will hop, run, or swim away. But it has another, more powerful weapon if this fails. All amphibians have special poison-producing glands in their skin. In many cases, this poison gives the creature a nasty taste but is not otherwise dangerous. A few species, such as the family of arrow-poison frogs of South America, are deadly. One tiny drop of their poison is enough to kill a monkey instantly. Like many poisonous creatures, these frogs are boldly colored to warn predators.

YOUNG FROGS
The female strawberry arrow-poison frog looks after the tadpoles while they develop into adult frogs.

1. The eggs are laid on a leaf.

2. When the tadpoles hatch, they wriggle onto their mother's back.

3. She carries them to a leaf-pool, high up a tree, where they can grow into frogs.

Giant toad
The warty lumps on this toad's skin are glands full of poison. Its flesh is poisonous too.

GRANULAR ARROW-POISON FROG
Shown at actual size—about 1 inch

Granular arrow-poison frog
This tiny frog lives in the tropical rain forests of South America. Despite the frog's small size, its venom is so toxic it can kill many people. Local tribes use its poison to coat the tips of hunting arrows and blow-pipe darts, creating lethal weapons.

Amphibians cannot inject their poison into an attacker. Instead they release poison through ducts in the skin, making their bodies taste nasty.

Although arrow-poison frogs are some of the most poisonous species known to humans, they are preyed upon by the frog-eating snake, which appears to be immune to their poison.

All arrow-poison frogs are boldly colored to warn predators to keep their distance. Some frogs are a brilliant green color. Others are black and yellow, gold, pink, or deep red and blue.

Spiny newt
If a spiny newt is grabbed by a predator, such as a bird, it sticks out its long, sharp ribs. They pierce poison glands in the newt's skin, and poison squirts into the bird's mouth, causing it terrible pain.

Spotted salamander
When attacked, this salamander bends its neck, which is filled with poison glands, toward an attacker so that, if bitten, it will taste unpleasant.

37

Spiders

Spiders are famous for spinning silk webs, which they use to trap insects and other small creatures such as woodlice and centipedes. Once the prey is caught, the spider kills it by injecting venom into it through sharp-tipped, hollow fangs. All spiders have a poisonous bite, but out of the 30,000 species of spiders only about 30 are dangerous to people. These include the funnel-web spider and the black widow spider. The black widow is found in many parts of the world, but only the larger female is dangerous to people. The much smaller male's fangs are not strong enough to penetrate human skin. The funnel-web was thought to be the most venomous of all spiders, but scientists now think that several other species may be more poisonous, such as the Brazilian wandering spider.

The biggest spiders are the tarantulas, or bird-eating spiders. Tarantulas are peaceful creatures and will only bite if seriously provoked. Even then, their bite is not usually fatal to humans. As with most spiders, tarantulas prefer to scurry away rather than stay and fight.

Black widow
One of the deadliest of all spiders, the black widow is capable of killing a person with a single bite. It is greatly feared because it often lives near people's homes. However, it is a shy creature and will usually attack only if something disturbs it.

Trapdoor spider
This spider digs a burrow in the ground, with a trapdoor made of silk, sometimes mixed with earth or plant material. The spider waits behind the door until an insect walks by and then rushes out, killing the insect with a poisonous bite. Some spiders locate prey by holding the door ajar, while others spin silken threads to trip up prey.

Funnel-web spider
The funnel-web is one of the world's most dangerous spiders. This deadly creature lives in Australia, where it often digs its burrow in people's gardens. It has a poisonous bite that causes sickness, severe pain, and muscle spasms, and can kill a person in less than two hours unless he or she is quickly treated with antivenom.

A spider injects its poison through a pair of hollow, curved fangs in the front of its mouth. The poison trickles into the fangs from special poison glands in the head.

If caught in the open, funnel-web spiders adopt an aggressive pose by raising their front legs and exposing their formidable-looking fangs.

As their name suggests, funnel-web spiders spin funnel-shaped webs. These lead into their underground burrows, built beneath rocks or logs. If a creature walks across the web, the spider senses the vibrations and rushes out for the kill. Funnel-webs eat insects, frogs, and lizards.

FUNGI

There are more than 50,000 species of fungi, including many different types of mushrooms, toadstools, molds, and mildews. Fungi used to be classed as plants, but they are so peculiar that scientists now consider them as a group of their own. They have no leaves, flowers, or roots, and do not make their own food as green plants do. Instead they feed on dead or living matter, sucking up its goodness through a mass of tiny threads, known as hyphae.

Some types of fungi are very useful. The life-saving antibiotic penicillin, for example, comes from the penicillium mold. Some mushrooms and toadstools are good to eat. But some, such as the death cap, are deadly poisonous. They may look harmless but they cause death quickly if eaten. Never pick fungi to eat, however sure you are of their identity. It is far safer to buy them from a shop or supermarket.

Roll rim
The roll rim is a very common fungus that grows in the fall in conifer forests and mixed woodland, especially near birch trees. It has a yellow-brown cap, which can measure more than four inches across, with a characteristically rolled-up edge. It grows to a height of about three inches. The roll rim is highly poisonous.

FUNGI LIFE-CYCLE
Fungi do not reproduce with seeds, as most plants do. Instead they produce millions of tiny spores that grow on ridges, known as gills, underneath the cap. The spores are released into the air to be carried by the wind. If they land in a suitable place, they begin to grow into a network of threads, or hyphae, known as a mycelium. This part of the fungus lives for years under the ground. Some of the hyphae mesh together to form a button-shaped fungus, which pushes above the surface. It grows into a fungus identical to the parent.

1. Spores are dispersed in the air.

2. The spores begin to grow into hyphae.

3. The hyphae fuse together to form a mycelium.

4. A small button-shaped fungus forms and pushes above ground.

5. The button-shaped fungus is protected by a covering known as a veil.

6. The veil ruptures and an adult fungus grows.

40

Pink crown

Orange peel

Death cap

The death cap is one of the deadliest of all fungi and is capable of killing a person. Even a chunk smaller than a sugar lump can be fatal. This fairly common fungus grows in the fall, under beech and oak trees. It is also found in parks and even in gardens. It has a white stem with a pale, yellowish-green cap. Older death caps smell strongly of cheese. More people are poisoned by death caps than by any other type of fungi. This is because they are sometimes mistaken for other fungi, which look similar but are edible.

Cup fungi

The orange peel fungus and the pink crown fungus belong to the group of brightly colored, cup-shaped fungi. Orange peel fungi look like ragged scraps of orange peel lying on the ground in the late fall and winter. They are yellowy-orange on the inside, growing mainly in conifer woods. Pink crown fungi grow in woods, half-buried in the ground. They are pink on the inside and white on the outside. Cup fungi are poisonous but can be made edible by boiling. They must never be eaten raw.

Fly agaric

Fly agarics have bright red, saucer-shaped caps with white spots and a white stem. They grow in the fall in woods, mainly under birch or pine trees. Like their relatives, the death caps, fly agarics are extremely poisonous and should never be picked. Small amounts can cause unconsciousness and even death. These fungi grow up to eight inches tall and can measure up to six inches across their caps.

OCTOPUSES

Octopuses live in oceans all over the world, even in the coldest waters of the Arctic and Antarctic. They all have eight legs but range in size from 2 inches to 30 feet. Many octopuses can move about very quickly by means of jet propulsion (drawing water into their bodies, then shooting it out again). When threatened, they shoot out a screen of black ink, which gives them time to make their getaway. Octopuses can also change color very rapidly to blend in with their surroundings and to show their mood.

All octopuses have a poisonous bite, which they use to paralyze and kill their prey. But octopuses are extremely shy and will attack people only if they are provoked. They feed on crabs, clams, shrimp, and fish and will sit and wait for hours for suitable prey to pass by.

Octopus briareus
This octopus paralyzes crabs with its poisonous saliva. It can gather as many as 25 crabs at a time in its long tentacles.

Common octopus
The common octopus can change color very quickly to blend in with its surroundings and so hide from its enemies.

BEARING YOUNG
Octopuses mate in winter. The female lays her eggs under a rock and guards them until they hatch several weeks later.

1. The adults mate.

2. The female guards her eggs.

3. The babies hatch (shown in closeup).

Octopuses hold their prey firmly in their sucker-covered tentacles, then bite the prey to inject a lethal nerve poison.

Blue-ringed octopus

This octopus lives along the coasts of Australia. It is small—just six inches long including its tentacles—but it is one of the world's deadliest creatures. Its poisonous bite can kill a human within five minutes. If provoked or threatened, the blue-ringed octopus flashes its bright-blue markings as a warning. Then it bites!

The octopus has a large brain and good eyesight, which help it while hunting.

GLOSSARY

Allergic
Unusually sensitive to such things as insect bites and stings, pollens, or certain foods.

Amphibians
A group of cold-blooded animals that live both on land and in water. They include frogs and newts.

Antibiotic
A medicine used to treat infections, such as pneumonia, caused by bacteria. The antibiotic penicillin comes from the penicillium mold, a tiny fungus.

Antivenom
A medicine used to treat people who have been bitten by a poisonous animal. Venom is another word for poison; "anti" means against. If an antivenom is given soon enough, it neutralizes the poison and may save a person's life.

Aphids
Small insects, such as a greenfly, that live in large numbers on plants, often causing damage.

Barbed
Describes an object or creature that is covered in tiny, sharp points. Animals and plants use barbs for self-defense.

Camouflage
A disguise used by many animals that makes them difficult to see. Camouflaged animals use colors, special patterns, and shapes to help them blend in with their backgrounds.

Cartilage
A gristly, elastic material that makes up the skeletons of sharks, rays, and skates instead of bone.

Cocoon
A silky case spun by an insect larva to protect itself while it changes into an adult.

Coral
A hard substance made of limestone. It is formed by tiny marine animals called polyps as an external skeleton. As the polyps die, their skeletons build up to form coral reefs.

Echinoderms
A group of marine animals including sea stars, sea urchins, and sea cucumbers. Many have hard, spiny skins.

Fangs
Long, hollow teeth, sometimes adapted for injecting poison into a victim.

Fatal
Something that is likely to cause death.

Hibernation
When an animal hibernates, it sleeps all winter. It does so because food is scarce and it might starve otherwise.

Insects
The largest group of animals. An insect's body is divided into three parts: a head, thorax, and abdomen. Insects usually have a pair of antennae, three pairs of legs, and one or two pairs of wings.

Larva
The young of an insect that often looks very different from the adult insect. For example, a caterpillar is the larva of a butterfly.

Lethal
Capable of causing death.

Mammals
A group of animals that breathe air, have hair and earflaps, are warm-blooded, have backbones, and look after their young, feeding them on milk.

Mimic
To copy or imitate. Many harmless plants and animals look like poisonous ones so that browsers and predators will leave them alone.

Mollusks
A group of animals that includes mussels, squid, octopuses, and snails.

Monotremes
Mammals that lay eggs (unlike most mammals, which give birth to live young). There are only two types—duck-billed platypuses and echidnas.

Nervous system
The system that controls an animal's movement and senses, such as touch, sight, and hearing.

Paralyze
To damage an animal's nervous system so that it cannot move or breathe properly but is still alive.

Parasite
An animal or plant that lives on another animal or plant and gets its food and nourishment from it without giving anything in return.

Poisonous
Poisonous animals or plants produce harmful chemicals to kill their prey or to defend themselves. The poison is administered through bites or stings, or is found in an animal's skin or flesh.

Predator
An animal that hunts and kills other animals for food.

Prey
Animals that are hunted and killed by other animals for food.

Quills
The hard, hollow spines that cover a porcupine's body.

Reptiles
A group of animals that includes snakes, lizards, crocodiles, and turtles. They are cold-blooded, have scaly skin, and most live in warm areas.

Rodents
The group of mammals that includes porcupines, guinea pigs, chinchillas, rats, mice, squirrels, and beavers. They have large, sharp front teeth used for gnawing their food and for digging.

Salivary glands
Parts of the mouth that produce saliva (spit). Some animals have poisonous saliva for killing their prey.

Serrated
Something that has jagged edges.

Species
A particular type of animal or plant. Members of the same species can mate and produce young that can have young themselves.

Spores
Tiny, seedlike specks from which new fungi and plants such as ferns grow.

Tentacles
Long, slender "limbs" used by an animal for feeling, grasping, or moving.

Venomous
Another word for poisonous.

INDEX